The
Tall Man
from
Boston

Marion L. Starkey

The Tall Man from Boston

illustrated by Charles Mikolaycak

CROWN PUBLISHERS, INC., NEW YORK

Inquiries should be addressed to Crown Publishers, Inc.,
419 Park Avenue South, New York, N.Y. 10016.
Manufactured in the United States of America
Published simultaneously in Canada by General Publishing Company
Limited
First Edition

The text of this book is set in 12 pt. Caslon 137.
The illustrations are pencil drawings reproduced in halftone.

Library of Congress Cataloging in Publication Data

Starkey, Marion Lena.
    The tall man from Boston.

    SUMMARY: An account of the Salem witch trials emphasizing the
role of John Alden, one of the unjustly accused "witches."
    1.   Witchcraft—Salem, Mass.—Juvenile literature.
[1.   Witchcraft—Salem, Mass.]   I.   Mikolaycak, Charles.   II.   Title.
BF1576.S82 1975   133.4'09744'5   75—9970   ISBN 0-517-52187-3

The
Tall Man
from
Boston

Today in Salem it is fun to play at being a witch. It is most fun of all on Hallowe'en, when the children go out to ring doorbells and cry "Trick or Treat!" Boys dress up as wild Indians or even as devils. Girls put on long skirts, shawls, and tall hats, and say they are witches. It is great fun.

However, nearly three hundred years ago, devils and witches were not fun. Salem people believed in 1692 that witches were destroying them. And though no one was playing trick or treat, young girls had much to do with this fear.

There were then two Salems, Salem Town and Salem Village. The town was a busy seaport with shaded streets and pleasant houses. About six miles inland was the other Salem. At first it was called The Farmers, then Salem Farmers, and finally Salem Village.

The Tall Man from Boston

8

About five hundred people lived there in ninety households. Most of their farms were in widely scattered clearings among the forests. They were God-fearing folk, and since it was hard to follow the rough trails to get to Sunday meeting in Salem Town, about twenty years earlier they had been given permission to build a meetinghouse of their own.

Their church became the center of the village. It was built near the green, where the men could march and train with their muskets on muster day. At one end of the green stood the watch house, built of logs in a day when people feared Indian attacks. Not far away stood the minister's parsonage and a few homes. The biggest building was the inn, or Ingersoll's Ordinary as it was called. Ingersoll was a deacon in the new church, a good man, who on a cold or rainy Sabbath invited the church-goers to take their ease between services before the fire-place in his comfortable rooms.

In 1692 about a dozen girls became famous in Salem Village. The homes of some were close to the meeting-house. Others lived farther out. During this winter most of them had one thing in common: they found life dull.

No fun and games were planned for them. There were no dances, no holiday festivals. Even Christmas was forbidden by the stern Puritans. In the shut-in months of winter, life became especially dull.

For their brothers, winter had its pleasures. They could vary their chores by helping their fathers at the trades many farmers turned to when planting and reaping were done. They could learn cobbling or tray making. Best of all, on good days they could borrow their fathers' muskets or fishing lines to try their luck on birds and deer in the woods or fish under ice in the creeks.

The girls had plenty to do in winter. They could bake and cook. They could spin and weave and sew and help their mothers care for the latest babies. But this was shut-in work. There was no adventure in it. They craved a change, they craved fun.

And some of them found it in, of all places, the parsonage.

The minister, Samuel Parris, had once been in business in the West Indies. When he came back he brought with him two servants, John Indian and his wife, Tituba.

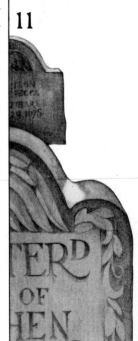

Some say these were black slaves, some that they were
Carib Indians. Whichever they were, Tituba loved to
spin tales, and, if the girls begged her hard enough, she
would tell their fortunes.

What would their parents have said, or the minister,
if they had known that the girls were going to the parsonage to get their fortunes told? Today's parents would
have laughed. But at that time, fortune telling was
thought to be a great sin, a dealing with the devil himself. The girls knew that and took pains to see Tituba
only when the minister and his wife were nowhere about.

Two members of the minister's family shared their
secret. These were the daughter, eight-year-old Betty,
and the eleven-year-old niece, Abigail Williams. Abigail
loved keeping a secret from the grown-ups. Betty did
not. When her father preached of the devil and hell, she
could not hold back her tears. She knew that what the
girls were doing was wicked. She knew that it was even
more wicked not to tell her parents.

Why did she not? One reason was her love for Tituba. She had seen her father beat Tituba when he was unhappy with her. Betty wept when it happened. She couldn't bear to get Tituba into worse trouble.

Another reason was Abigail. Abigail had always bossed her around and did so now. She would do dreadful things to Betty if Betty told her mother about the fun they were having in the kitchen.

Soon, though, the burden became too great for so little a girl. She began to cry out in her sleep. One morning when her father led family prayers, she covered her ears and fell screaming to the floor.

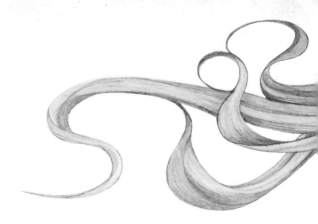

The Tall Man from Boston

Then Abigail became ill. With her, it was a noisy illness. A time was coming when her uncle would find it nearly impossible to preach a sermon above the racket that Abigail was making. Yet he did not punish her, for by then he was certain that an evil hand was upon Salem Village.

The sickness spread to the older girls. They knew as well as Betty that what they were doing was wrong and if discovered would bring severe punishment. One by one they fell into fits so strange that the whole village was aroused.

Good Dr. Griggs was called in. He had never seen a sickness like this. He had no name for it and no remedy. At last he said what people had feared he would say, "The evil hand is on them."

What did he mean? The evil hand was the work of witches. And what were witches? They were people who turned from God to do the devil's bidding. For this the devil gave them the power to harm people they didn't like, such as these poor girls.

Not quite everyone believed Dr. Griggs, but most people did, especially the girls. The explanation, however, did not cure them. Instead, being told that the devil was after them frightened them even more and increased their illness. They were now in a pitiful state.

What was to be done? Find the witches, of course, and put them out of the way. But how to find them?

People looked to the girls. Could they not see the witches who hurt them so? Surely God in His mercy would open their eyes. So they turned to the girls and asked again and again, "Who afflicts thee? Poor child, who afflicts thee?"

The girls had no answer. Later they would name half the colony of Massachusetts, but at first they named no one. They did not know the cause of their illness. They were sorely hurt, but they could not see who hurt them.

A new way had to be tried. The grown folk asked each other who in the village was most likely to be a witch. They thought of old quarrels with their neighbors.

The
Tall Man
from
Boston

19

The Tall Man from Boston

It was a village of many quarrels. The farmers disputed with each other about where their boundaries lay. Sometimes two families would come to blows in a wood-lot that both claimed. They blamed each other for not keeping their fences tight, so that horses and hogs got through to each other's gardens.

Worst of all, they quarreled about their church. So far they had had four ministers. No matter who was chosen, there were always some who claimed that another choice would have been better. None of their ministers had lived happily in Salem Village.

Thinking such thoughts, they put new questions to the girls. Not "Who afflicts thee?" but "Doth so-and-so afflict thee?" When they did this, the eyes of the girls were opened one by one. They had visions. They began to see in their mind's eyes those named to them. They cried out these names and the arrests began.

The first three taken as witches were people whom no one liked, and one of these was Tituba. Before Tituba was taken to court her master gave her a whipping. His aim was to beat the truth out of her.

Did Tituba try to tell him that the girls came to her to have their fortunes told? If so, he didn't believe a word of it. He beat her until she told him what he wanted to hear, that she was a witch and that she and the other two had put their marks on a book the devil had in which to record the names of those who promised to serve him.

Tituba, in short, "confessed." That is, she told the court what it wanted to hear. And she frightened everyone when she said how many names there were on the devil's book. There were nine. Since she could not read, she could not tell who they were. But they were some people she had seen. One was what she called a Tall Man from Boston.

The arrests went on. Now good church members were brought to court. One was Martha Cory, who dared to say that she did not believe in witches. Another was Rebecca Nurse, a seventy-year-old grandmother whose neighbors loved her (all but one—Rebecca had once had harsh words for a neighbor whose hogs had ruined her flax patch).

But the officers of the court were troubled. Who was that Tall Man from Boston whom Tituba had seen? They could not rest until he was found.

Again, they asked the girls. The girls said that they saw a tall man clearly. He came to them often to choke them. But they did not know his name. How could they? None of these simple village maidens had ever been to Boston. They could name no man there, short or tall.

Again the grown folk had to take action. They consulted each other. Of what tall man in Boston had they heard gossip? They tried one name on the girls, and soon one of them called it out in her fits. The name was John Alden.

The first John Alden came to Plymouth on the *Mayflower*. When his friend Miles Standish asked his help in courting Priscilla, he did his best until Priscilla said, "Why don't you speak for yourself, John?" So John married Priscilla, and this John Alden was their son.

He still considered his birthplace, Plymouth, as his real home. But business often took him to Boston and he had a fine house there. He was also a tall man.

When he was told to go to Salem to face the girls, he at first refused. He was a busy man. Often he was at sea with one of his ships. Lately he had been in Maine helping Governor Phips put down an Indian uprising. What he had heard of what was going on in the two Salems struck him as nonsense. He wanted no part of it and refused to go.

Then he got a direct order. It came from William Stoughton, who was acting as governor while Phips was away in Maine. When Stoughton said "Go," you went.

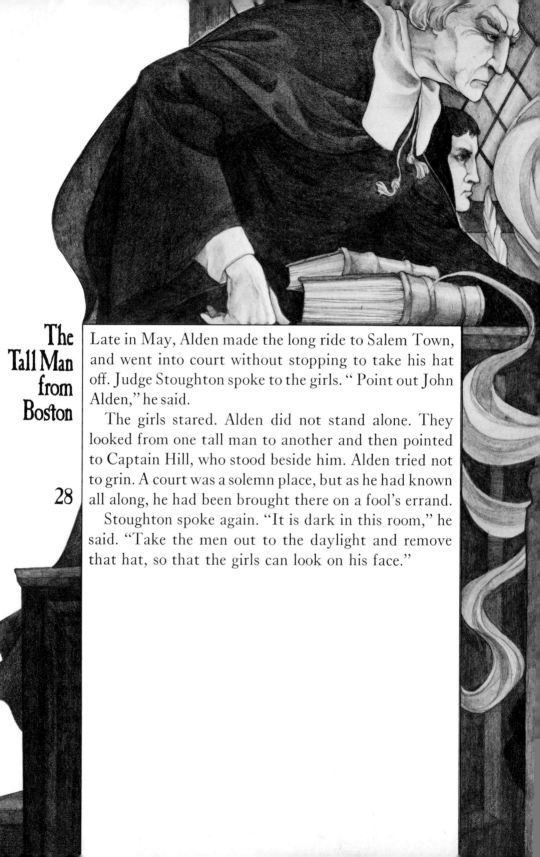

The Tall Man from Boston

Late in May, Alden made the long ride to Salem Town, and went into court without stopping to take his hat off. Judge Stoughton spoke to the girls. "Point out John Alden," he said.

The girls stared. Alden did not stand alone. They looked from one tall man to another and then pointed to Captain Hill, who stood beside him. Alden tried not to grin. A court was a solemn place, but as he had known all along, he had been brought there on a fool's errand.

Stoughton spoke again. "It is dark in this room," he said. "Take the men out to the daylight and remove that hat, so that the girls can look on his face."

Outside the girls had no doubt.

"There stands Alden!" cried one. "A bold fellow with his hat on before the judges."

Another, who had heard gossip, added more. "He sells powder and shot to the Indians and French and lies with Indian squaws and has Indian papooses."

John Alden was angry. "There is not a word of truth in what they say of me!" he cried. What was true was that he had stood before the judges with his hat on. Back in court, hat in hand, he faced the judges.

"Now just why," he asked, "do your honors suppose that I have no better things to do than come to Salem to afflict these persons that I never knew or saw before?"

The judges made no reply. They had been blamed for judging good people on evidence no better than dreams. Now they had found one sure test. They called it the touch test.

Alden was told to stand before the court with his face turned to one side while the girls were brought in. When they arrived, he was told to look at them.

As his eyes met those of the girls, they screamed and fell to the floor. There they lay howling, twisting their limbs into strange positions.

This was the first part of the touch test. No order could have been heard above the bedlam the girls were making, but the officers knew what to do. One by one they lifted the girls from the floor and guided their right hands to the right hand of John Alden. When that was done, most of the girls fell quiet and could stand without help.

What had been done? No one explained at the time, but Alden learned later that the people believed that his eyes had sent witch poison into the girls and the touch of his hand had drawn it back.

Even Alden had been startled, but he kept his wits about him. When it was quiet in the court, he tried a test of his own. He turned to a good friend who today sat with the judges.

"I look at you now," he said. "Will you fall in fits?"

It was a good question. What explanation could there be that his friend did not fall? But there was no answer. The friend had come to help Alden. Now, having seen what he had seen, he believed him guilty.

"Confess and give glory to God," he said sternly.

"I hope to give glory to God," replied Alden, "but not to gratify the devil. I wonder at God in suffering these creatures to accuse innocent people."

No one believed him. He hoped to make a better case when he was brought to trial before a jury. What had happened today was only an examination to see if there were cause to hold him for trial. Alden had failed his test and he was held.

Most people were held for trial in jail. But by now the jails in both Salem and Boston were terribly over-crowded. (There was even one five-year-old "witch" in the Boston jail.) As a man of high place, Alden got special treatment. He was put under house arrest in his Boston home.

The Tall Man from Boston

36

Here he sat for most of a long, hot summer. Some of his friends visited him. Judge Samuel Sewall came to pray with him. But as the trials went on, Alden had small faith in the prayers of even a friendly judge.

The judges were hanging everyone who came before them, even one minister. Salem Village had always quarreled with its ministers. When one of the girls saw George Burroughs in her fits, he was arrested in Maine, taken to court in Salem, tried and hanged. What hope was there for Alden, if a minister could not prove his innocence?

Even more frightening was what happened to Rebecca Nurse. At her trial the jury brought in a verdict of Not Guilty. Chief Justice Stoughton would not accept it. He sent the jury back to think it over, and this time they came back saying Guilty.

What hope was there for rough-and-ready John Alden, if a good old grandmother, who in her own words "never afflicted no child, no, never in my life," was hanged?

How could he defend himself? There was one way, the way Tituba had found. It was to confess, to tell the judges not the truth but what they wanted to hear.

Many people were doing that now, and they were not hanged. The judges could not do without them. They did not accept a confession until the confessor named other witches he had seen. That was how the minister, Burroughs, had been convicted. Not only the girls, but also many of the confessors said they had seen him at the witches' sabbaths serving red wine and red bread to the devil.

Those who told the truth got hanged. They were heroes. The cowardly liars were let off.

Was John Alden a hero? It took a great deal to frighten him. He had stood on his ships unafraid before gales. He had stood unafraid before Indians and their arrows. But now he was afraid.

Searching his Bible he found a queer text, "Better a living dog than a dead lion." It was not a text he liked but it was Holy Writ, and as time went on it made sense.

The Tall Man from Boston

The Tall Man from Boston

Alden had a trusted friend in a town near Plymouth. One night this friend was roused from sleep by a pounding on his door. When he opened it, there stood John Alden.

"The devil is after me!" cried Alden, and his friend took him in.

No one was hunting witches in little Plymouth. If young girls there had fits and cried out on their neighbors, they were spanked and sent to bed without their supper. The Tall Man from Boston was safe as long as he kept away from Boston.

In the spring he was able to return.

Strange things had happened since Alden had run for his life. Governor Phips had come back from Maine to find the whole colony in an uproar. A judge had left court in anger at the way the trials were going. A local officer had refused to make any more arrests. The girls were calling out the names of the judge, the officer, and even of Lady Phips, when she tried to help a friend.

At the risk of their lives, country people were signing petitions that they knew no evil of some of those arrested. Ministers were protesting the tortures used on prisoners. Husbands were demanding that their wives be taken from jail and sent home.

Governor Phips put a stop to the trials. After September there were no more hangings.

In January the trials began again, but in a new way. Dreams, fancies, and the touch test were no longer accepted as evidence. There had to be physical proof of wrongdoing, and there was no such proof.

Under the old rules, the judges could find no one innocent. Under the new, they could find no one guilty.

In the spring the governor issued a general pardon for those accused and not yet tried. Thinking people now knew that a great wrong had been done.

The Tall Man from Boston

Judge Sewall, who had prayed with John Alden, stood up in church and asked to be forgiven for condemning the innocent. So did the whole witch jury. So in time did one of the girls, Ann Putnam.

The colonial legislature passed a law pronouncing many of the condemned innocent and paying their families for their expenses. The legislature could not bring the dead back to life, but it brought comfort to many families. No longer need they live in shame as the kinfolk of criminals.

As for the Tall Man from Boston, John Alden was long back at home, when he wasn't on one of his ships or off on an Indian campaign. He lived a long and useful life.

The Tall Man from Boston

All this took place in the very distant past, nearly three hundred years ago. Yet it is not forgotten. What was then called Salem Town is now spoken of as Witch City.

Salem Village, where all the trouble started, is not even on the map. Not long before the American Revolution, when the village became a town, it took a new name. To find where most of the village stood, look for Danvers. Why this name, no one quite knows. And one corner of Salem Village has yet another name. It is Peabody.

Today, wherever you go, in Salem, Danvers, or Peabody, it would be hard to find a child who lives in fear of witches.

To children today, witches are something they read about in fairy tales. They are figures of fun, and that is why on Hallowe'en they can dress up as witches and go from house to house calling "Trick or Treat!"

Yet, what is fun today was no fun at all in 1692.

for Chloe and Nina

Marion L. Starkey is the author of *The Visionary Girls*, which was an ALA Notable Children's Book. She has also written adult books on the Salem witchcraft trials and is regarded as an expert in this area of American history. This is her first book for Crown.

Charles Mikolaycak is a well-known illustrator of children's books. His illustrations for *How Wilka Went to Sea and Other Tales from West of the Urals*, Translated and Edited by Mirra Ginsburg, are receiving praise everywhere.